CHRISTMAS SONGS

Arranged by Chad Johnson

T0081330

ISBN 978-1-4803-9452-0

HAL•LEONARD®
CORPORATION

7777 W. BLUEMOUND RD. P.O. BOX 13819 MILWAUKEE, WI 53213

Visit Hal Leonard Online at
www.halleonard.com

The Chipmunk Song

Words and Music by Ross Bagdasarian

The Christmas Song
(Chestnuts Roasting on an Open Fire)

Music and Lyric by Mel Tormé and Robert Wells

Do You Hear What I Hear

Words and Music by Noel Regney and Gloria Shayne

Feliz Navidad

Music and Lyrics by José Feliciano

Frosty the Snow Man

Words and Music by Steve Nelson and Jack Rollins

Have Yourself a Merry Little Christmas

from MEET ME IN ST. LOUIS

Words and Music by Hugh Martin and Ralph Blane

Here Comes Santa Claus
(Right Down Santa Claus Lane)

Words and Music by Gene Autry and Oakley Haldeman

A Holly Jolly Christmas

Music and Lyrics by Johnny Marks

(There's No Place Like)
Home for the Holidays

Words and Music by Al Stillman and Robert Allen

Jingle Bell Rock

Words and Music by Joe Beal and Jim Boothe

The Little Drummer Boy

Words and Music by Harry Simeone, Henry Onorati and Katherine Davis

Merry Christmas, Darling

Words and Music by Richard Carpenter and Frank Pooler

The Most Wonderful Time of the Year

Words and Music by Eddie Pola and George Wyle

Silver Bells

from the Paramount Picture THE LEMON DROP KID

Words and Music by Jay Livingston and Ray Evans

White Christmas

from the Motion Picture Irving Berlin's HOLIDAY INN

Words and Music by Irving Berlin

NOTES FROM THE ARRANGER

Arranging for three ukuleles can be challenging because of the instrument's limited range. In standard tuning (G-C-E-A), there is only one octave plus a major sixth between the open C string and fret 12 on the A string. Certain melodies easily span this distance and more, so compromises sometimes had to be made.

Not all ukuleles have the same number of frets. If your uke has fewer than 15 frets, you may need to play certain phrases an octave lower (especially in Part I). Some phrases have already been transposed up or down an octave—this was only done out of necessity and kept to a minimum. A few songs require every inch of available fretboard, but fret 15 on the first string (high C) is the limit, and this is extremely rare.

The three voices will sometimes cross as a result of range limitations. If Part III is considered to be the "bass" line, keep in mind that the lowest available "bass" notes are sometimes on the first string! However, if you own a baritone ukulele, almost all of the notes in Part III could be played an octave lower (except the open C string and C♯ on fret 1), thus providing a more effective bass line.

Despite the above caveats, I believe that the spirit of these songs has been preserved, and I hope you enjoy playing these arrangements as much as I enjoyed creating them. By the way, a fourth ensemble part can be added by strumming along with the chord symbols!

– Chad Johnson

SOPRANO, CONCERT & TENOR FRETBOARD

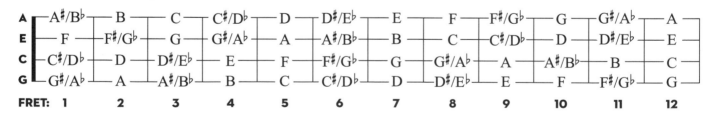

BARITONE FRETBOARD

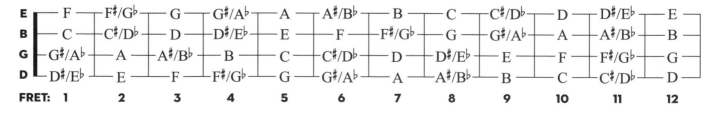